Freedom, Peace, and Unity

Freedom, Peace, and Unity

Arthur Dick

Published by Arthur Dick
PO Box 84177 RPO
Calgary, AB T3A 5C4
Canada

ISBN: 978-1-7781489-0-3

First Edition

Visit the author's website at arthurdick.com.

Contents

Dedicated to the people of Ukraine.

Nightingale Interrupted

The nightingale sang in the silence
of a peaceful Ukrainian forest.
I heard the nightingale's melody.
Singing of love
in a peaceful world,
a world without violence,
but its melody is no longer heard.

In this forest,
the song of the nightingale is interrupted
by the thundering of war machines.
Now the nightingale is silent.

The nightingale's song will not be heard
in this war-torn forest.
I hear only the deafening roar of war,
and what remains of the nightingale
is a sad song.

But the nightingale's song
was not in vain—
because the world has heard it.
The world will remember the nightingale.

Shadow of War

The great grey beast has awoken;
the wings of war are beating.
The great grey beast is destroying
all the good, snuffing out the light.

You look for peace and find war,
you look for life and find death,
you look for the light and find darkness.

The great grey beast is tearing
thousands of dreams apart;
the great grey beast is pulling
the bright flowers from the ground.
Night is falling
on the fields of Ukraine.
The deceit of great grey beast
has covered the sky with darkness.

But the people are not silent.
In the dark of the night
they are building bright towers
to the heavens.

The stars are blinking,
and listen to the people singing:

“We need peace now!
We need to end this war!
Our army is fighting for freedom!”

The great grey beast is flying,
but the voice of the people
is rising above;
and they will not be afraid.

Come, sing a song of peace;
sing for freedom, love, and joy.
Sing a song of hope,
a melody for a bright future.

The great grey beast is dying;
it's letting out one last roar.
After the night
comes the first light of morning.

The Machine

Chainsaw tears the heart to dust,
then whistling rustling leaves.
They believe they're virtuous,
we're falling on our knees.

Giants left as lifeless stumps
and a vagrant herd of deer,
who from their newfound grass abyss
watch cattle drawing near.

The noxious poison cloud of mist
descends from up on high,
but they only targeted the pests,
poor swooping dragonfly.

Disembowelling iron claws
unearthed the wriggling worm.
Machinery has drained the swamp:
dust swirls up in return.

They claim they're not the ones to blame,
for following the plan.
These furious flames ignited now,
no one can understand.

Shattered Pyanska

A shattered pyanska lies on the ground,
its pieces strewn across the battlefield,
and crushed into the dirt
by soldiers' boots.

This once colourful country,
now blackened by war.
Its people fighting and dying
for their right to self-determination.

We must stand together
and put an end to this fighting.
We must stop the aggression
and defend Ukraine's integrity.

Let us come together
and paint new beautiful eggs.
Let them shine brightly in the sun,
for Ukraine and for all people.

The Use of Propaganda

The forces of evil use propaganda
to disguise their footprints;
the good, to lift the veil.

The forces of evil use propaganda
to wage war;
the good, to keep peace.

The forces of evil use propaganda
to destroy our future;
the good, to build a better tomorrow.

The forces of evil use propaganda
to roil the waters;
the good, to fish truth from the depths.

The forces of evil use propaganda
to control and enslave;
the good, to unify the world.

The Call to Truth

The roar of social media
and the smear of fake news
are a call to arms.

A call to stand up and show the world
that we know the truth.
That there is nothing fake
about our commitment to truth.

The tactics deployed by the enemy
to manipulate the consciousness,
to control minds,
and spread their propaganda
are limitless and endless.

There's no substitute for truth
and we refuse to give in
to fabrications and lies.

We're not going to be fooled,
and we're not going to be silenced.

This is the dawning of a new age
where truth is being awakened
and no one can hide
behind a book filled
with lies and deceit.

A new day is dawning.

So hold strong.
Stick to the truth,
and keep the flame alight.

And Yet Again

And yet again the sky is red,
and yet again the blood is shed.

And yet again the mountains crack,
and yet again the tanks attack.

And yet again the earth quakes,
and yet again the body aches.

And yet again the evil dream
ignores the words that people scream.

And yet again the gods throw dice,
and innocents will pay the price.

And yet again the voice of peace
is calling for the clash to cease.

And yet again, and yet again ...

Stop the War

We are watching in horror
as the fire of war
spreads across Ukraine,
while the rest of the world sleeps.

The invaders are cruel
and hostile, as they try
to destroy the land's people.

They want to steal the sovereignty
and hollow out the land,
destroy history's remnants.

Blood is on their hands,
and hatred fills their hearts.

We need to stop the war;
to build a new world
in which we are all equal,
with the love of mankind.

We must unite and fight
to douse the fire of war.

War has no future,
its embers will grow cold.

Revolution

War is a king on the throne,
and we the lowly peasants,
who dream of a better life.

But even the king is mortal,
and there will come a time,
when we tear down the king's walls
and the king will be dethroned.

Hark! What sounds are those?
The clashing of steel?
No, it's the clanging
of a thousand anvils.

The smithing of a new day.

Let the fires of creation
burn through the night,
and forge a new world.

The people will live in peace,
and no one will dream of war,
because we'll have the world,
and the world will be ours.

War will be but a memory,
and peace will reign.

The World is One

The world is one,
though we have chosen to divide it.
We have drawn lines in the sand,
and built walls to keep each other out.

But the world is one,
and we are all its people.
We are brothers and sisters,
mothers and fathers,
sons and daughters.

We are one,
and we must work together
to make the world a better place,
to make the world one again.

As we are one,
let us begin.

The New Beginning

Demons in the minds of men
stand poised to unleash
the fires of destruction again.

The terror incited
by the shroud of its baleful shadow
boils like a storm above the world.

We cannot run from this threat,
and we will not hide.
We will stand and fight.

The end we seek
is to create a world
without war or terror.

We must embrace a new beginning.
We must unite hands and hearts.

We will walk together into a tomorrow
where we honour each other's dignity.

We will not be adversaries,
but partners and friends.

And when our work is done
we will know peace.

The Breadbasket

In a world of war,
food is the ammunition.
The breadbasket is the battlefield,
and the dinner table is the front line.

Children are the casualties,
their bellies swollen with hunger.
Families are torn apart,
searching for a scrap to eat.

But one day,
this will all be over.
And on that day,
we will feast.

A Call for Peace

O, Ukraine, betrayed by Russia,
how you are forsaken.
Your land laid out with coffins,
with the bodies of your brothers.
The blood of the war
has turned your fields crimson.

Your enemies are cruel and unrighteous,
they have robbed the people,
they have killed them.
They want to drown you in blood
and seize your beautiful land.

We don't need war,
we don't need death,
we don't need blood and hatred.
We need peace, we need freedom,
we need truth and justice.

Ukraine, Ukraine, we love you.
We want to live with you, to grow with you,
to sing and laugh with you,
to build our future together.

Ukraine Will Prevail

There's a seed within the ground,
but the seeds of ills are older.

There's a flower above the grass,
but the flowers of peace are lovelier.

There's a star above the sky,
but the stars of truth are brighter.

There's a din above the silence,
but the song of the people is louder.

There's a sword above the shield,
but the shield of Ukraine is mightier.

There's a dream within the darkness,
but the dream of Ukraine will prevail.

Ukraine, Land of Golden Fields

Let the heavens be covered with a rainbow,
let it look like a shining bead.
Let the joyful sun shine,
let it make the land fertile.
Let the farmers sow their grain,
so the whole Ukrainian land becomes golden.

Let the imperialists stay in their corner,
and the nationalists stay in their hole.
Let the fakers stay in their place,
among the corrupt and the restless.
Let the Russians stay in their country,
while the Ukrainian people live on their land.

Let the politicians stay in their government,
and the diplomats stay in their offices.
Let the army stay in their bunkers,
and put criminals in their cells.

Let the beautiful Ukraine be free!
Let the whole world live at peace!
Let's live and love each other.
Let's build a better world.

Let the people join together,
and grow a productive crop.
Let the people live in harmony,
and in freedom, reap the harvest.

United We Stand

We, the friends of the Ukrainian nation
stand in solidarity with you
as you struggle with the Russian bear.

We are your friends.
We stand with you
to protect our common values.
Through the storm and the sleet,
we will never leave you.

We are with you, people of Ukraine.
We stand together in the struggle.
Joined in spirit, today and beyond the horizon.
We stand together,
knowing freedom is not free.

The flame of freedom, which the people
of Ukraine have ignited, will burn brightly.
We will dance in its light.

Oh, Ukraine, we see your strife!
We will overcome all
that is evil and darkness,
as long as we hold to love.
We will overcome
as we join hands
to create a better day.

The Nightingale

Though small and weak,
the nightingale does not bow
to the strikes of the eagle.

A great and powerful,
but sinful and unprepared eagle.

Nightingale, make your voice heard
against the war,
and against all aggression.

Sing so loud that the eagle
will not hear the sound of its own wings.

The eagle attacks
but does not understand its fate
is hanging on a small nightingale's voice.

Oh, sing and sing,
for a peaceful future.
The song of the nightingale will never end.

A Sunflower Story

Sunflowers. Ukrainian land is filled with them.
For the sunflower to grow and prosper,
to develop and flourish,
people must have love and care,
to give it attention.

We sow the seeds of love,
slowly and carefully,
so that all of us,
can safely, securely,
enjoy the blessings of tomorrow.

Let's come together and sow,
so that the sunflower of healing,
of compassion, of peace,
can grow high, and together,
like a family, with our hands, and hearts,
we will create a better future.

The future is a sunflower,
that all people, from all nations,
can look up to and see.
A future we all believe in,
and we all can share.

Requiem for Fallen Sunflowers

The Ukrainian flag flies in the sky.
The sunflower's petals lay on the ground.
The people gave their lives for freedom.
They loved their country and they loved their land.

Snow falls, covering flowers;
frost covers the ground.
Petals fall from flowers,
and the people are not silent.

Their cries for peace echo in the land.
They chant "Peace."
They chant "Peace."
They chant "Peace."

Their voices can be heard across the land,
and they will not be silenced.
Their voice will echo until the land is free.
Their voice will echo until the land is free.

Strength of Love

We are the unwanted, unloved, and forgotten,
but we will never give up.
This is the revolution
of forgiveness, compassion, and strength.

When the darkness closes in
we sing songs of hope and courage,
we tell stories of happiness and love
until the sun shines brightly again.

Like leaves in the forest,
like the snow in winter,
or stars that shine in the night,
we resist the fight with our strength of love.

Someday we will rejoice together
the music will swell with joy
and peace will settle upon us,
for love is the strongest force of all.

Ukrainian Rose

The Ukrainian people
have been through so much pain and suffering,
and like the rose,
they still manage to bloom and grow.
Their resilience is amazing.
No matter how much they are attacked,
they always find a way to survive.
Their strength is an inspiration to us all.

They are a reminder that no matter how dark
and cold the world may be,
there is always hope for a better tomorrow.
Their courage is a shining light in the darkness,
and we must never forget their sacrifice.

The Ukrainian people are a rose
that will never be forgotten.

Children of Peace

War is a malignant sickness
that gnaws
at the heart of mankind
and degrades
all those who take part in it.

The scars of war don't heal.
Not for the soldiers
who gave their lives for nothing.
Not for the families
who lost loved ones.
Not for the children
who have to live with that pain.

The ripples of war spread out
and touch
every corner of the world.

A smoke-filled sky
blots out the sun.
When the dust clears,
children of peace
will be standing there
shining their light
and singing their song.

www.ingramcontent.com/pod-product-compliance
Ingram Content Group UK Ltd.
Pitfield, Milton Keynes, MK11 3LW, UK
UKHW020421250726
13967UKWH00007B/2754

9 781778 148903